One World

On the Move

Valerie Guin

A+
Smart Apple Media

Note
about the series
One World is designed
to encourage young
readers to learn more
about people and places
in the wider world. The
photographs have been
carefully selected to
stimulate discussion
and comparison.

First published in 2004 by Franklin Watts
96 Leonard Street, London EC2A 4XD

Franklin Watts Australia
45-51 Huntley Street, Alexandria, NSW 2015

This edition published under license from Franklin Watts. All rights reserved.

Copyright © 2004 Franklin Watts.

Editor: Caryn Jenner, Designer: Louise Best, Art director: Jonathan Hair, Map: Ian Thompson
Reading consultant: Hilary Minns, Institute of Education, Warwick University

Acknowledgements: Adrian Arbib/Still Pictures: 12. Bob Battersby/Eye Ubiquitous: 23b. Nigel
Cattlin/Holt Studios: 6. James Davis Worldwide: 16b, 18t, 22, 23t. Bennett Dean/Eye Ubiquitous: 21.
Mark Edwards/Still Pictures: 17. Robert Francis/Hutchison: 16t. Angela Hampton/Ecoscene: 10.
Jeremy Horner/Hutchison: 8. Luc Hosten/ Ecoscene: 19. Oldrich Karasek/Still Pictures: 11. Robert
Landau/Corbis: 9. Ray Moller: 7. NASA: 27. NASA/Eye Ubiquitous: 26. Edward Parker/Hutchison:
14. Joe Pasieka/Eye Ubiquitous: 13t. Christine Pemberton/Hutchison: 13b. Harmut Schwarzbach/Still
Pictures: 15. Paul Thompson/Eye Ubiquitous: 24. Isabella Tree/Hutchison: endpapers, 2, 3, 25. Nick
Wildman/Eye Ubiquitous: 18b. Michael S. Yamashita/Corbis: 20.

Published in the United States by Smart Apple Media
2140 Howard Drive West, North Mankato, Minnesota 56003

U.S. publication copyright © 2006 Smart Apple Media
International copyright reserved in all countries. No part of this book may be reproduced in any
form without written permission from the publisher.
Printed in the United States of America

Library of Congress Cataloging-in-Publication Data

Guin, Valerie.
On the move / by Valerie Guin.
p. cm.
ISBN 1-58340-699-9
1. Transportation—Juvenile literature. I. Title.

TA1149.G85 2005
629.04—dc22   2004052503

9 8 7 6 5 4 3 2 1

Contents

Getting around

People all around the world
need to **travel** from one place
to another. They use many
ways to get around.

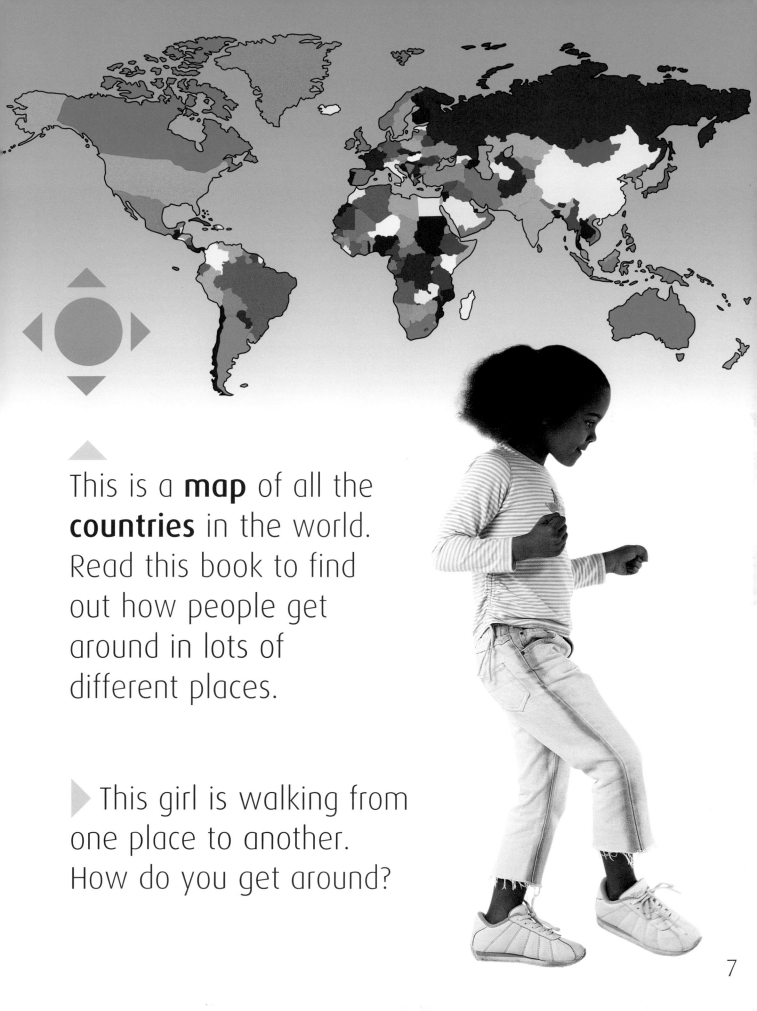

This is a **map** of all the **countries** in the world. Read this book to find out how people get around in lots of different places.

▶ This girl is walking from one place to another. How do you get around?

Cars

In some places, cars fill the roads. This traffic jam is in the **city** of Bangkok in Thailand. There are more than two million cars in Bangkok.

In the **countryside**, where fewer people live, there are fewer cars. This road is in Italy.

Bicycles

People often ride bikes for fun. These children are biking on a special bike path in the United States.

In many countries, people bike to work. These people are riding their bikes to work in Chengdu, a city in China.

Riding animals

In Mongolia, people ride horses to get around. Families often own a whole herd of horses, and children learn to ride when they are very young.

In the desert of Sudan, people often ride camels. A camel can travel a long way across the dry desert without needing a drink.

Most elephants in Nepal are wild. But some elephants are trained to carry people and **goods**.

13

Boats

These people in Peru live in small **villages** around a lake. They use a boat to travel. The man at the front pushes the boat through the water with a long pole.

People can take their cars across the water on this ferry in Kenya. The ferry ride is much shorter than driving all the way around by road.

Buses and trolleys

People in Panama can get around on colorful buses called *chivas*.

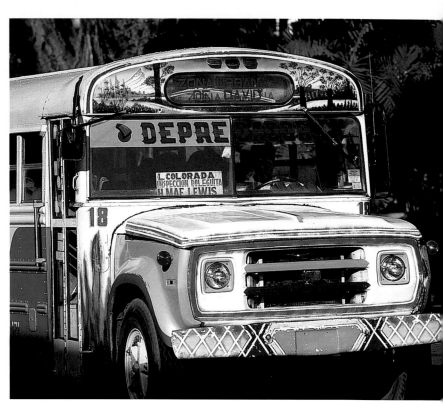

In Britain, people ride on double-decker buses. Passengers climb the stairs inside the bus to get to the top floor.

In cities like Amsterdam in the Netherlands, people can take trolleys to get around. Trolleys run on tracks through the streets.

Trains

This bullet train zooms past Mount Fuji in Japan. The bullet train is one of the fastest trains in the world.

Underground trains, or subways, are a quick way to get around in cities. This one runs in Moscow in Russia.

This steam train in South Africa carries tourists across the steep hills and valleys, so they can see the beautiful countryside.

▼

Delivering things

These boats are carrying bricks down the Grand Canal in China. The Grand Canal is a man-made river. Boats use the canal to carry goods from place to place.

This road train carries goods across long **distances** in Australia. The driver sits in the truck at the front, which pulls the trailers along the long empty roads—like a train without tracks.

Going for a ride

▶ Instead of roads, the city of Venice in Italy has canals filled with water. People ride around the city in boats called gondolas.

In the city of Rio de Janeiro in Brazil, people can take a cable car up to the top of Sugar Loaf Mountain.

During the snowy winters in Norway, people can go for a ride in a dog sled.

In the air

An airplane flies powerfully through the sky. It can carry people across long distances very quickly. This airplane has just taken off from an airport in Spain.

A hot-air balloon drifts slowly through the sky. The passengers in this hot-air balloon in Namibia are looking for wild animals.

In space

It's lift off! Rockets launch the space shuttle into the sky. The rockets give the shuttle extra power to fly into space, then they drop away.

In space, astronauts travel high above the Earth in the space shuttle orbiter.

All around the world

All over the world,
people use many
ways to get around.

United
States

Brazil

Panama

Peru

The countries that you
have read about are
shown in pink on this
map of the world. Find
the country that matches
each picture in the book.

Britain

Netherlands

Norway

Russia

Mongolia

Japan

China

Spain

Italy

Sudan

Nepal

Thailand

Kenya

South Africa

Namibia

Australia

Glossary

city   a large town where many people live and work

countries   places with their own governments

countryside   land that is natural without many houses

distances   the space between places

goods   things that are bought and sold

map   a drawing that shows where places are located

travel   to move from one place to another

villages   small towns, usually in the countryside